Multiethnic CONVERSATIONS FOR KIDS

Mark DeYmaz and Oneya Fennell Okuwobi

ILLUSTRATED BY CHARLOTTE C. BLACK

wesleyan
PUBLISHING HOUSE
wphstore.com
Fishers, IN

Copyright © 2022 by Wesleyan Publishing House
Printed in the United States of America
Published by Wesleyan Publishing House
13300 Olio Road, Suite 100
Fishers, Indiana 46037

ISBN: 978-1-63257-512-8
ISBN (e-book): 978-1-63257-513-5

Library of Congress Control Number: 2022942419

CONTENTS

JESUS PRAYED FOR US

In prayer, we share our deepest thoughts and feelings with God. When we are feeling upset or scared, our prayers are extra important. So, imagine Jesus as He was about to go to the cross. Although He knew what He needed to do, He was worried about what would happen. What do you think His big prayers were? What might have been on his mind?

We actually don't have to guess, because John 17 tells us. He prayed with all his heart for us to be one. He wasn't asking for us all to become one person—it's certainly not possible to squish us all together! Instead, He was focusing on the idea

> Father, I pray they will be one, just as you are in me and I am in you. I want them also to be in us. Then the world will believe that you have sent me. I have given them the glory you gave me. I did this so they would be one, just as we are one. I will be in them, just as you are in me. This is so that they may be brought together perfectly as one. Then the world will know that you sent me. It will also show the world that you have loved those you gave me, just as you have loved me.
>
> *—John 17:21–23*

of unity. Unity means being joined together in purpose—sort of like a sports team working together to win a game. Jesus and God the Father are the perfect example of unity. They care about the same things. They agree with each other on everything. Jesus even said that He doesn't do anything unless He sees His Father doing it!

Jesus prayed that everyone who believes in Him would be just as united as He and His father are. And He gave us a big promise in this prayer: If we are united—if we act, think, and live as one—the whole world will believe in Jesus! Unfortunately, we are not always united. Too often, even people who love Jesus use their differences to stay separate in all sorts of ways.

For example, people come in many different skin colors. This is because people long ago lived in different places—some hotter and some colder than others. God designed melanin to protect people's skin who lived in hotter places. More melanin makes a person's skin darker and more protected from the sun. Less melanin makes it lighter and less protected. Hair also helps protect people from the sun. Thick, curly hair protects more than thin straight hair does. Over time, some people noticed differences in hair and skin and divided people into groups they called races. Because of this, many have treated the groups differently, being kinder to some and meaner to others. We often have separate churches based on these differences too. This has kept us from being one. We have let other things keep us from being united too, such as what country we are from, our culture or way of doing things, and even how much money we have.

This is not what Jesus prayed for.

Jesus and God the Father are the perfect example of unity.

That's why this book exists. As you read, have conversations with your grown-ups about how we can all come together. You can read a chapter every night for twenty-one nights or three chapters a week for seven weeks. Either way, as we explore Bible stories about being one, we will learn how to bring unity even with differences. By doing this, we have a part in being the answer to Jesus' prayer!

KNOW

WE ARE DIFFERENT PARTS OF THE SAME BODY

Together, the people all over the world that follow Jesus are one body. We are not an actual, physical body, but God wants us to work together, exactly like the parts of a body. The fact that we are one body doesn't mean everyone is the same. In a body, all the parts are different, but they work together to get the job done. What would it be like if eyes tried to be a different body part? Eyes are great for seeing, but they wouldn't do a very good job as stomachs or feet! It's the

Suppose the foot says, "I am not a hand. So I don't belong to the body." By saying this, it cannot stop being part of the body. And suppose the ear says, "I am not an eye. So I don't belong to the body." By saying this, it cannot stop being part of the body. If the whole body were an eye, how could it hear? If the whole body were an ear, how could it smell? God has placed each part in the body just as he wanted it to be. If all the parts were the same, how could there be a body? As it is, there are many parts. But there is only one body. The eye can't say to the hand, "I don't need you!" The head can't say to the feet, "I don't need you!"

—1 Corinthians 12:15–21

same with the Church as the body of Christ—if we try to make everyone the same, nothing will work very well.

Too often, the people who gather together for church are all the same in some way. Perhaps they are from the same country, like Korea or Mexico. Perhaps they are all the same race, like Black or White. Maybe they all live in the same neighborhood and work at jobs that are alike. When this happens, we end up trying to smell with feet, because we don't have all the parts of the body. We miss what people who are different from us can offer.

Instead, we can all get to know people who are different from us in some way. We can learn what they do well and show them what we do well. An arm on the ground by itself isn't very useful; arms work very well connected to a body. We are better together!

LET'S TALK ABOUT IT

1 What is something special about you? What do you have that you could teach someone else?

2 What body part do you think you might be in the Church? For example, I might be an eye, because I see things others might miss, or I might be a mouth, because I love to sing.

BE

LOVE WELL

In the New Testament book of Galatians, we learn about the fruit of Spirit, which includes nine characteristics the Holy Spirit helps followers of Jesus grow in their lives. The fruit of the Spirit is love, joy, peace, patience, kindness, generosity, faithfulness, gentleness, and self-control. In some of our readings, we will talk about these characteristics. Today, we will talk about love. If we are loving, people can believe God is too.

If we say that Jesus loves everybody, but we do not love other people, especially people that are in some way not the same as us, our words make no sense. Our words are like a noisy gong and people will not pay attention to what we have to say about God. . . . But the best thing you can do to help others believe in God and feel welcomed in the church is to love them just like Jesus loves them, no matter who they are, what they look like, or from where they've come.

—*1 Corinthians 13:1, 13 (paraphrase)*

A man named Paul once wrote about love in a letter he sent to people living in a city named Corinth. These people, called Corinthians, believed in Jesus and went to the same church. When Paul's letter arrived, they read it together.

Many ships sailed to and from Corinth. In fact, ships were coming and going from its harbor day and night, bringing food, clothes, furniture, and more to the city from faraway lands. On these ships were sailors and passengers from many different places in the world. They were men and women, old and young, rich and poor. Because they were from different places, they did not all speak the same language, and they had different ways of doing things. Many different kinds of people came to live and work in Corinth because of these ships. And the church in Corinth was made up of different sorts of people too.

Even though they all loved Jesus, Paul wrote his letter because he wanted to make sure they all loved each other too.

Why was it important to Paul that the Corinthians loved each other even though they had differences in their age, culture, and country of birth? Paul knew that if everyone did not love each other, other people living in the city might not believe their message that "God loves all people." When we demonstrate genuine love for all people, not just some people, we make Jesus happy. When the way we act matches what we say, we make it easier for others to believe in God too.

LET'S TALK ABOUT IT

1 Why do you think it's important to be friendly with other people that might not look like you at school, on the playground, or at church?

2 Is it hard to talk to people different from you or to be their friend? Why or why not?

DO

COMMIT TO UNITY

Paul wrote letters to Christians living in many different places. He wrote these words to people living in a city called Ephesus. Like the Christians in Corinth, Christians in Ephesus were also

> For this reason, I too, having heard of your faith in the Lord Jesus and your love for all the saints, do not cease giving thanks and praying for you.
>
> —*Ephesians 1:15–16*
> *(paraphrase)*

people of many different countries and cultures. But that didn't stop them from loving each other. They were patient and gentle with one another. In fact, everyone in the church in Ephesus was committed to unity and peace, despite their differences. That's why Paul was so proud of them—and he told them so. Their faith in Jesus changed their minds. Their love for Him made loving one another possible.

Once, a certain man asked Jesus, "What is the most important thing God wants me to do?" Jesus told the man to love God with all his heart and to love his neighbor in the same way he loved himself. According to the Bible, a "neighbor" is not just someone that lives nearby or someone that we sit next to at school. A neighbor could also be someone very different from us (see Luke 10:25–37). It's someone that might be hard for us to like or get to know at first. Through his many letters, Paul encouraged Christians not only to love and serve Jesus, but to love and serve one another. Wherever they did, many others came to believe that Jesus was God and Savior of the world.

LET'S TALK ABOUT IT

1 Do you find it hard or easy to love yourself? If you felt about yourself the way God feels about you, how would you feel?

2 Do you find it hard or easy to love others? How about others who seem different from you?

DO! What is a country (other than the US) where you have been or that sounds like a fun place to go someday? With your grown-up, look up information about people living in that country. Find out what language people living in that country speak; what foods they like; and what kinds of clothes they wear. What else is unique about the country you chose? Draw a picture with the information you found.

INCLUDE OTHERS

Jesus often did something that drove His disciples crazy. He hung out with people that good Jewish people had been taught not to hang out with. An example of this was his conversation with a Samaritan woman. At that time, Jewish people would do anything to avoid Samaritans, even walking two days further, if necessary, to avoid the area of Samaria! What's more, women and men who were not related usually avoided talking together in public. Five different husbands

Jacob's well was there, and Jesus, tired as he was from the journey, sat down by the well. It was about noon. When a Samaritan woman came to draw water, Jesus said to her, "Will you give me a drink?" (His disciples had gone into the town to buy food.) The Samaritan woman said to him, "You are a Jew and I am a Samaritan woman. How can you ask me for a drink?" (For Jews do not associate with Samaritans. Jesus answered her, "If you knew the gift of God and who it is that asks you for a drink, you would have asked him and he would have given you living water."

—*John 4:6–10 (NIV)*

abandoned this woman, so even the people in her own town didn't want to talk to her. That is why she was drawing water by herself at noon, when the sun was very hot.

Jesus did not care what anyone said about who He talked to. He knew that this woman was God's child, and He knew that talking to her was God's plan. He spoke to her with kindness, helping her learn the truth about God. Near the end of their conversation, He told her that He was God's Son—something not even His disciples were sure of yet! This conversation had an amazing effect. The Samaritan woman ran into her town, excited and yelling, "Come, see a man who told me everything I ever did. Could this be the Messiah?" (John 4:29 NIV). People in her town, people who wouldn't even talk to her before, listened and came to meet Jesus. That day, many people heard God's Word. Because of this, many Samaritan people later became Christians.

> Jesus did not care what anyone said about who He talked to. He knew that this woman was God's child.

When churches exclude people, they are leaving out those who could share God's Word with others. When we exclude people, we are ignoring those who Jesus loves. If we want to be like Jesus, we must be willing to treat everyone with respect and care, even if others expect us not to. We must learn to include everyone equally.

LET'S TALK ABOUT IT

1 Have you ever seen someone left out at recess or lunch? How could you help that person feel included?

2 Have you seen some groups of people be more ignored than others, like the Samaritans were? Why do you think that is? Is there anything you can do to help?

3 Do you sometimes feel left out? How can you remember that God loves you even when you feel ignored?

BE

BE A PEACEMAKER

T he second fruit of the Spirit we will learn about is peace. Jesus tells us that people who make peace are blessed. In fact, He says

> Blessed are the peacemakers, for they will be called children of God.
>
> —*Matthew 5:9 (NIV)*

peacemakers will be called God's children! We all want to be in that category. But how do we make peace? Well, the answer may surprise you.

Sometimes to make peace, we must start with disagreement.

There is a difference between *keeping* peace and *making* peace. Peacekeepers want to prevent fighting, so they avoid bringing up areas of disagreement. The result is that there is no real unity. People keep their feelings and opinions to themselves, and neither side knows what the other is thinking. Peacemakers, though, bring the disagreement to everyone's

attention, so that people can talk about it and work it out. That way everyone can move forward together.

Archbishop Desmond Tutu, a peacemaker in South Africa, once said, "If an elephant has its foot on the tail of a mouse and you say that you are neutral, the mouse will not appreciate your neutrality." A peacekeeper might want to stay neutral and not say anything in the situation. They might not want to take sides. After all, mice are quiet, and elephants are loud. People may be happier not talking about the poor mouse's tail, because mice can't complain that much. But that is not true peace. Peacemaking happens when someone speaks up to tell the truth about how the mouse is being hurt—and then makes it right. Speaking up creates lasting peace, because once truth is known, everyone can have a future where their tails are safe!

1. Is it hard for you to speak up when it might lead to a disagreement? Why or why not?

2. Can you think of a situation in which you could become a peacemaker? What would you need to speak about?

DO

SHARE POWER

In those days the number of believers was growing. The Greek Jews complained about the non-Greek Jews. They said that the widows of the Greek Jews were not being taken care of. They weren't getting their fair share of food each day. So the 12 apostles gathered all the believers together. They said, "It wouldn't be right for us to give up teaching God's word. And we'd have to stop teaching to wait on tables. Brothers and sisters, choose seven of your men. They must be known as men who are wise and full of the Holy Spirit. We will turn this important work over to them. Then we can give our attention to prayer and to teaching God's word." This plan pleased the whole group. They chose Stephen. He was full of faith and of the Holy Spirit. Philip, Procorus, Nicanor, Timon and Parmenas were chosen too. The group also chose Nicolas from Antioch. He had accepted the Jewish faith. The group brought them to the apostles. Then the apostles prayed and placed their hands on them. So God's word spread. The number of believers in Jerusalem grew quickly. Also, a large number of priests began to obey Jesus' teachings.

—Acts 6:1–7

That's not fair!

Maybe you've heard a younger brother or sister or a friend at school yell that when things weren't going well. Maybe that's even been your own cry when you weren't being treated the same as someone else. The truth is, sometimes people are treated unfairly based on the way they look, who their family is, or many other reasons that just aren't right. What can we do when this happens? The first thing is to believe the people who are crying, "Not fair." The non-Greek Jewish people had the power in their group because they had been the leaders. They could have said to the Greek Jews, "Why are you complaining? That's not true!" Instead, they did not argue. They believed the Greek Jews when they said, "That's not fair!"

The second thing they did was to fix the problem by sharing leadership. The non-Greek Jews knew that they couldn't fix the problem while they were still the only leaders. So, they shared power with the Greek Jews, making them leaders in the church too. We know this because Stephen, Philip, Procorus, Nicanor, Timon, and Parmenas are all Greek names! From then on, the Greek Jews oversaw one of the most important things the church did—feeding widows. The Christians of that time were so known for feeding widows that the Roman people, who usually didn't like Christians, gave them praise saying, "These Christians feed not just their widows but ours too!" Because of their generosity, many people admired the church.

1 When was the last time you heard someone complain about something not being fair? Did you believe them? Why or why not?

2 Why is it important to believe someone who complains about unfairness? How should we respond?

DO! Make a list of the leaders in your church or your school. Are there any groups left out of leadership? Imagine what sharing power might look like.

KNOW

TELL OTHERS ABOUT JESUS

When we are young, we need older people to explain things we don't understand. Maybe your mom or dad, grandma or grandpa, or another adult helps explain things to you. These grown-ups love you. They want you to a become a smart and happy person so someday you can help other people too. At school, teachers also help us learn things we do not yet know. They enjoy seeing us become all that God created us to be.

One of the early Christians, whose name was Philip, went to a city in a nation called Samaria and told many people about Jesus. These people, called Samaritans, were not like Philip who was a Jew. They did not believe the same things as the Jews did about God. But when the crowds heard Philip speak about Jesus, they paid close attention to what he said . . . and many of them began to live for Jesus.

—*Acts 8:5–6 (paraphrase)*

The fact is that all of us, even grown-ups, need people like parents and teachers in our lives. Why? Because there's not one person alive that knows everything! Philip was an older man who knew a lot about Jesus. He was living his life to make God happy. He loved to tell others about Jesus. Philip knew that God loved everyone no matter what they looked like or where they were from. He wanted all people, not just some people, to believe in Jesus. He wanted Samaritans, as well as his own Jewish people, to experience God's love and believe. That's why Philip left his own country to go to another country and tell people about Jesus. That's why he went to Samaria and spoke with the Samaritans. Maybe someday you will want to go to another country to tell people about Jesus and learn from them in return. But think about it: you don't have to go to another country to help others learn more about God. You don't even have to be older than you are right now to do so! You can share what you already know about God with others. When you tell others about Jesus, you make God happy. You help them understand how much He loves them. That's what Philip did—and you can too!

LET'S TALK ABOUT IT

1 Who first told you about Jesus? What did they teach you about Him?

2 Who is someone you know that might need to know about Jesus? How might you help that person know more about Jesus and His love for them?

3 If you could go to another country to tell people about Jesus and learn from them in return, where would you like to go and why?

BE

BE PATIENT

The third fruit of the Spirit we will focus on is patience. When we are patient with others, we display God's character. Earlier in his letter to the church at Ephesus, Paul explained that Jesus lived His life, died on a cross, and rose from the grave. Jesus did this so that anyone and everyone who believes in Him will one day go to heaven. In part, this is what makes us Christians—our faith and hope in Jesus to give us the gift of salvation. This means that if we believe Jesus is God, we will someday live with Him forever in a real place called heaven. Plus, we get to help spread the good news

> I, Paul, urge all of you in the church at Ephesus to walk together in unity, in a manner that pleases God. To do so, you will have to be humble, gentle, and patient with one another. You will also have to make sure that at all times you love one another well, remain unified in spirit, and committed to living together in peace.
>
> —*Ephesians 4:1–3 (paraphrase)*

about God on earth (see Eph. 1:3—2:9). Paul also explained that, while we are alive on earth, anyone and everyone who believes in Jesus should feel welcomed and included in the Church (see Eph. 2:10—4:6). In fact, Paul expected that Christians would do all they could to make sure that this happened. Why was this so important to Paul? At the time in which Paul lived, some Jewish people who believed in Jesus thought that only people who were like them could someday go to heaven. They also thought churches were just for Jewish people who believed that Jesus was God. But Paul, although he too was Jewish, knew that God loved all people, not just some. Since anyone and everyone who believes in Jesus and confesses their sins will someday go to heaven, Paul wanted anyone and everyone to be part of a church, so that they might learn more about Jesus, how much He loves them, and someday go to heaven with us!

Paul wanted anyone and everyone to be part of a church . . .

How can we help to make all people, not just some, feel welcomed and included in church? Paul told us to be gentle and patient with everyone in the church; to love people well by being kind; and to be a peaceful person that helps others get along. When we do such things, we make God happy. We help others know and feel God loves them too.

1 Have you ever gone somewhere new and felt that people there were not nice to you? If so, how did that make you feel? Did you want to go back?

2 What do you think it means to be gentle and patient with people?

3 How can you be nice and kind to others in your neighborhood, at school, or in church?

DAY
9

DO

LEARN FROM PEOPLE OF OTHER CULTURES

Ethiopia is a country in East Africa. It is also home to one of the first groups of Christians in the world. When an Ethiopian eunuch, a high-ranking official of the queen, met Philip (yes, the same Philip who talked to the Samaritans), the eunuch was reading the book of Isaiah. This book is found in the Hebrew Scriptures, also known as our Old Testament. Books were very expensive at that time, so this eunuch had made a huge investment in reading God's Word. As the eunuch read, Philip explained that the passage he was

> And as they were going along the road they came to some water, and the eunuch said, "See, here is water! What prevents me from being baptized?" And he commanded the chariot to stop, and they both went down into the water, Philip and the eunuch, and he baptized him. And when they came up out of the water, the Spirit of the Lord carried Philip away, and the eunuch saw him no more, and went on his way rejoicing.
>
> —*Acts 8:36–39 (ESV)*

reading referred to Jesus. This man believed and was baptized right away!

Not only was he baptized, but he also went back to Ethiopia and spread the good news about Jesus everywhere. People became Christians. Then even more people shared the good news through trading routes around the country, and Philip's message was confirmed. We have proof of this. Historians have found a church building in Ethiopia dating way back to the fourth century.[1]

> One of the most important things the Ethiopian Christians taught others was the importance of having the Bible in a language everyone could read.

Some people have been falsely taught that Christianity belongs to a certain group of people or countries. Learning about Ethiopian Christianity helps us know that this is simply not true. Jesus came to speak to all people—including rich people like the eunuch and poor people like Philip—Black people like the eunuch and Middle Eastern people like Philip. Each one of us is included in God's family. What's more, the Ethiopian church taught the global Church things that would help it mature. One of the most important things Ethiopian Christians taught was the importance of having the Bible in a language everyone could read. While other countries had Bibles in Latin that could only be read by religious leaders, the Ethiopians translated the Bible so everyone could read

God's Word. Martin Luther, a German church leader, learned from the example of the Ethiopian church and spread their way of doing things to the whole world. That's why we get to read the Bible for ourselves today in our own language!

LET'S TALK ABOUT IT

1 Why do you think we might not know much about Christianity in other countries?

2 What does it mean to you to be able to read the Bible for yourself because of the Ethiopians?

DO! With your grown-up, explore what Christianity looks like in another country. What do the Christians of that country give to all of us around the globe? What can we learn from them?

1. https://www.smithsonianmag.com/history/church-unearthed-ethiopia-rewrites-history-christianity-africa-180973740/

DON'T MAKE IT HARD TO FOLLOW JESUS

Throughout history, people have wondered: How is it possible to go to heaven just by believing in Jesus for salvation? Shouldn't we have to do something else, like give away our money to help needy people, or never do anything wrong, or in some other way prove to others we deserve to go to heaven?

Now in the early years of the church, some Jewish men who believed Jesus was God began teaching other believers, and specifically believers who were called "Gentiles" (that is, everyone who was not Jewish): "Unless you follow the laws of the Old Testament as explained by Moses," they said, "you cannot someday go to heaven." Though this was not true, many Gentiles were confused. So, the leaders of the church in Jerusalem came together to look into this matter. After there had been much discussion, one of the leaders named James stood up and said, "We who are Jewish Christians should not make it difficult for Gentile Christians to turn to God or be part of the church." In this way, then, the matter was settled and the whole church was happy with the decision.

—Acts 15:1–2, 6, 19, 22
(paraphrase)

It doesn't make sense that it would be that simple to go to heaven, but it is!

In fact, Jesus once said, "Because God so loved the world and all the people living in it, He sent Jesus from heaven to live with them, die for them, and rise again from the grave to prove that life after death is possible and that everyone who believes in Him will live forever with Him after they die" (John 3:16, paraphrase).

The book of Acts is one of many books in the Bible, and like every book, the book of Acts has an author. The author's name is Luke. Luke wrote the book of Acts to tell us how the first churches were started, why these churches were started, and about the many people from different backgrounds who first came to believe Jesus was God. These people became known as Christians (see Acts 11:26). We are also called Christians today, because we too believe Jesus was God.

How is it possible to go to heaven just by believing in Jesus for salvation?

Because the first Christians were from many different people groups, it was hard for them at first to trust each other and to agree about what they should all believe and how they should interact with one another in the church.

That's why what James said to the people in Acts 15:13 was so important. Since Jesus didn't make it hard for us to follow Him, we shouldn't make it hard for others to follow Him either. Because Jesus made it easy to be part of His family in heaven, we should make it easy for all kinds of people to be part of His family, the Church, on earth too!

LET'S TALK ABOUT IT

1 To believe that Jesus is God requires faith. To have faith means that you trust what someone says is true or that something will come true in the future, even though it hasn't yet happened. What is something you've done by faith or that you believe by faith will someday happen?

2 We learn to trust God, and we can also learn to trust each other. How can you learn to trust others who are different from you in some way?

BE

BE KIND

The fourth fruit of the Spirit we'll talk about is kindness. When you see someone that's hurting or in need, don't you want to help? I know you do—because I know you are a kind person! So . . .

- If you see a friend riding her bike down the street, but then she falls in front

Once, a man was walking down a dark street. Suddenly, robbers jumped out of the shadows, beat the man up, stole his money, and ran away. The man was so badly hurt that he was close to dying. Soon, two of his cousins traveled down on the same street. Even though they saw him lying on the sidewalk and crying out for help they did not stop. Instead, they hurried away. Later that evening, someone from a different country, a Samaritan, came upon the man too. Unlike the cousins, the Samaritan felt sorry for the man and decided to help. First, he used bandages to stop the bleeding and then he took the man to a nearby hospital. The Samaritan told the doctors to help the man and whatever the cost, he would pay the bill.

—*Luke 10:25–37 (paraphrase)*

of your house and starts to bleed, you'll go out and help her, right?

- If a friend of yours starts crying at school, you'll probably ask what's wrong and try to make him feel better. You wouldn't just walk away, would you?
- If someone you know is hungry, wouldn't you give them something to eat?

Whenever we help people, we are being kind, thoughtful, and compassionate. Being *kind* means that we are friendly, glad to help, and eager to share what we have with others.

Being *thoughtful* means that we think about how we would want to be treated if we were someone else—and then treat people that way. Being *compassionate* means that we care about others in ways they can see and feel.

Jesus is kind, thoughtful, and compassionate.

The Samaritan was a kind, thoughtful, and compassionate person. He felt sorry for the man that had been beaten and left on the road to die. It didn't matter to him that the man in the street was Jewish. The Samaritan said to himself, "The robbers could have hurt *me* instead and taken *my* money. If it was me lying there, I would want someone to help. So, I'm going to help this man!"

Jesus is like this. He is kind, thoughtful, and compassionate. It doesn't matter who someone is, where they come from, or what they have done in the past. Jesus is always thinking about and helping others. He expects us to be kind, thoughtful, and compassionate to others as well. When we help others in need, we do more than just tell people about God's love—we show them that God loves them. When we help others, we are being like Jesus. This makes Him happy, and it will make us happy too!

LET'S TALK ABOUT IT

1 How have you been kind or shown kindness to someone lately? (See the definition above.)

2 Have you ever looked at someone else and wondered what it would be like to be him or her? Tell me—what did you think or wonder?

3 Have you ever shown compassion to someone by caring for them in a way they could see or feel? What did you do and why? How did it make you feel?

DO

RECOGNIZE WE DO THINGS DIFFERENTLY

As we've learned, the people that follow Jesus all over the world make up one body. We can recognize that we all belong to God because of the Holy Spirit. As described in today's story from the book of Acts, some Jewish Christians did not believe that Gentiles could become followers of Jesus. They were proven wrong because the gift of the Holy Spirit was given to Gentiles too. But the discussion didn't end there. Once Gentiles became Christians, the Jewish Christians

"As I began to speak, the Holy Spirit came on them as he had come on us at the beginning. Then I remembered what the Lord had said: 'John baptized with water, but you will be baptized with the Holy Spirit.' So if God gave them the same gift he gave us who believed in the Lord Jesus Christ, who was I to think that I could stand in God's way?" When they heard this, they had no further objections and praised God, saying, "So then, even to Gentiles God has granted repentance that leads to life."

—Acts 11:15–18 (NIV)

began to try to change them and make them do things the way the Jewish Christians did.

When people come to Jesus from different cultures, they bring with them a lot of wonderful things. But sometimes, even today, the churches they come into try to change them. There may be a way that people expect others to worship or respond to the sermon or hang out with each other. When people don't act how others expect, they can be made to feel left out or like they need to change to fit in. When that happens, we don't really have the whole body. We miss what others can contribute because everyone is made to look and act the same.

> When everyone can be themselves,
> we are amazed at the different ways
> God works in each person's life.

For example, if your church service includes music, people may react differently to that music. Some people like to be loud and sing with all their hearts, lifting their hands, and even dancing to the music. Other people are quiet and may kneel or even begin to cry. If we tell the loud people to change, we will miss the happiness that comes from dancing for God without holding back. If we tell the quiet ones to change, we will miss the quiet peace that comes from just enjoying God's presence. When everyone can be themselves, we are amazed at the different ways God works in each person's life. What's more, when no one is left out, we also know that we can be ourselves too! This brings joy to us and to God, who made us just the way we are.

LET'S TALK ABOUT IT

1 Have you ever felt like you needed to change to fit in with your church community? How did that make you feel?

2 Think about the sentence, "Just because I'm different doesn't mean I'm wrong." What does it mean to you? How can we help other people feel that way too?

DO! Talk with your grown-up about how you are different from others you know. Write down some ways others are different from you and talk about how those differences are good.

DAY
13

KNOW

BE A FRIEND TO PEOPLE FROM OTHER CULTURES

When Peter, a Christian whose parents were Jewish, came to the city of Antioch, I, Paul, whose parents were also Jewish, had to boldly challenge him to change his behavior. Prior to other Jewish Christians arriving in the city, Peter would eat regularly with Gentile Christians; that is, with people who believed Jesus was God but whose parents were not Jewish. But when these Jewish Christians came to church, Peter stopped eating with the Gentile Christians. Peter was afraid that if he kept hanging around them, the Jewish Christians would say bad things about him. But Peter wasn't doing anything wrong: in fact, he was doing something right by hanging out with people from all kinds of different backgrounds! But not eating with the Gentiles was causing problems in the church, so I had to tell Peter to not avoid them. I told him from now on that he had to hang out with everyone who loved Jesus, not just the Jewish Christians.

—*Galatians 2:11–13 (paraphrase)*

Once, there was a man that loved watching birds. The more he watched birds, the more he learned about them and their differences. For instance, birds come in different colors, shapes, and sizes—and there are other differences too. Some birds, like eagles, fly in the air. Other birds, like chickens, do not fly much at all. Some birds live near water and like to eat fish, while others live in trees and like to eat worms. Also, different kinds of birds make different kinds of sounds. Like parakeets, for example—they chirp, and it sounds nice to our ears. But ducks—they quack. Their sound can be loud and annoying! There's something else the man noticed about birds. "Birds of a feather," he said, "flock together." In other words, birds that look and sound the same naturally want to be together. They feel safe when they're with other birds that are just like them. If you think about it, people are kind of like

birds. People come in different colors, shapes, and sizes too. Some people look the same, talk the same, and like to eat the same things. And like birds, people learn to want to be with others that are like them.

But our differences really shouldn't matter, because we are all people, and not birds. We don't have to be afraid of eating with different kinds of people, talking with others, or getting to know them. Unlike birds, we can choose to be friends with all kinds of people, and we should be their friends. Why?

Because every person is a human being that God created and loves. Since God is the one who created us, He loves every one of us just the same, no matter what we look like, talk like, or like to eat. God doesn't treat people differently based on the color of their skin or the shape and size of their bodies, therefore we shouldn't treat people any different than we want to be treated. Yes, God wants us to be friends with all kinds of people—and because God likes to be with all kinds of people, we should too!

LET'S TALK ABOUT IT

1 Why do you think it's important to be with all kinds of people?

2 When you think about your school, do birds of a feather flock together, or does everyone play with everyone else?

3 Name one way you can be a person who brings people from different cultures together.

BE

BE A GOOD PERSON

One time, a group of people, known as prophets, came down from the church in Jerusalem to visit the church at Antioch. Prophets are people with a unique, God-given ability to understand not only what's happening now but what will happen in the future. One of these prophets, named Agabus, stood up in church and predicted that a severe shortage of food, known as a famine, would soon spread over the entire Roman world . . . which later actually happened when a man named Claudius was the ruler of Rome. So, what did the followers of Jesus do in response? As each one was able, they decided to send money to help poor Christians living in Judea, the region in which the church of Jerusalem was located. Once the money had been collected, the leaders of the church at Antioch gave it to Barnabas and Saul, sending them to Jerusalem where they distributed it.

—*Acts 11:27–30 (paraphrase)*

Our fifth fruit of the Spirit to talk about is goodness.

Most people are good people. They are kind and tenderhearted. For example, if they know or see someone in need and asking for food, clothing, or money, they feel a desire to help. This should be especially true of Christians—those of us who believe Jesus is God. We know that God helped us by sending His Son, Jesus, to tell us about God's love. But Jesus didn't just tell us about God's love. He proved His love by dying for us, so that we might someday live with Him in a wonderful place called heaven. Because we know God helped us, we should want to help others also, especially when they're in need. God is good, kind, and tenderhearted, and we should be too.

But just because we feel a desire to help others in need doesn't always mean we actually do so. Why is that?

One reason is that helping others requires us to stop what we're doing, see others in need, and think about how we would want someone to think about us if we were in the same situation. For instance, what if you were hungry and didn't have any food. Wouldn't you want someone to stop what they're doing, recognize your need for food, and bring some food to you? It's easier for us not to help people in need, because it means that we have to stop what we're doing long enough to see them, think about them, and actually do something for them. It's also easier for us not to help people in need, because helping will usually cost us something. It may cost us time, money, or something we own because someone else needs it more than we do in the moment.

What the Christians in Antioch did was amazing! Instead of worrying about what might happen to them when the famine came, they worried more about others—the poor Christians living in Jerusalem. "What will happen to them if we don't help?" they asked. So, they gave away their own money to help. They did something good, kind, and tenderhearted, sending money to help others in need.

1 Have you ever helped someone in need? If so, what did you do? How did it make you feel?

2 The church at Antioch was filled with all kinds of people. They came from different places and countries. Not everyone looked the same or talked the same, but they all believed the same thing about Jesus. Why do you think it was easy for a church like this to think about others and act quickly to help poor Christians living in Jerusalem?

3 The truth is, we are all in need of something. What might someone in need have to offer you? What might you learn from them?

DON'T BE AFRAID TO SAY WHAT YOU'RE THINKING

This message is part of what King Lemuel's mother, who we know almost nothing about, wrote to her son. This wise woman instructed many things so that her son would live the way God expected. One of the most

> Speak up for those who cannot speak for themselves, for the rights of all who are destitute. Speak up and judge fairly; defend the rights of the poor and needy.
>
> —*Proverbs 31:8–9 (NIV)*

important things she taught was to speak up for others! King Lemuel's mother knew that as a king, her child could say just about anything and be listened to. The same was not true for everyone in the kingdom. There were some people in Lemuel's kingdom who were "destitute" or poor. It was very likely if they spoke up for themselves, no one would listen. King Lemuel's mother wanted to make sure that her son would always speak up for those who didn't have the power or position to speak up for themselves. The Bible calls this "righteousness" or seeking to make things right.

The truth is, we still have people not being listened to today. Scientists have done studies to show that White people are sometimes listened to more than people with darker skin. Sometimes men are listened to more than women. Sometimes rich people are listened to more than poor. None of this should be true. That's why we all have an important role. We can be good friends to those whose voices are not being heard by speaking up for what is right. What's more, instead of speaking for them, we can encourage others to listen to them.

For example, let's say that you play on a soccer team. One kid on your team always has holes in their shoes, and the other kids make fun and don't listen to them on the field. You can speak up. You can tell your team members that they aren't being fair. You can also set an example by listening to everyone equally yourself. If you speak up for others, that's a way you can be righteous and help make every place that you are better.

We can be good friends to those whose voices are not being heard by speaking up for what is right.

1 Have you ever seen someone not listened to, or have you not been listened to yourself? Why do you think that might have been?

2 Do you think it might be scary to speak up for others? How do you think you could face that fear?

DO! Do you know someone who is made fun of or isn't being heard because they are different? With your grown-up, brainstorm some ways you can stand up for them.

RICH ISN'T BETTER THAN POOR

One day, a friend of mine was at church. A person without a home wiped his snotty nose with his hand and then reached out that very same hand to shake my friend's. My friend did not hesitate for a minute. He shook the snotty hand with gusto, gave that man a genuine smile and struck up a conversation. He knew that being a friend to that man was more important than avoiding germs. This man without a home may have

> My brothers and sisters, you are believers in our glorious Lord Jesus Christ. So treat everyone the same. Suppose a man comes into your meeting wearing a gold ring and fine clothes. And suppose a poor man in dirty old clothes also comes in. Would you show special attention to the man wearing fine clothes? Would you say, "Here's a good seat for you"? Would you say to the poor man, "You stand there"? Or "Sit on the floor by my feet"? If you would, aren't you treating some people better than others? Aren't you like judges who have evil thoughts?
>
> *—James 2:1–4*

been met with disgust in other places, but that should never be true at church.

As much as poor people are sometimes met with disgust, rich people are often met with fascination. There have always been TV shows about rich people. A long time ago, it was *Lifestyles of the Rich and Famous*. Then after that came *Cribs*. More recently, programs like *Selling Sunset* showed us a life most of us can only imagine. We are fascinated by people who have fancy things. The apostle James saw that this fascination with wealth was happening even at church. People with fine clothes were given a good seat where everyone could see them. Poor people were given a place to stand or a seat on the floor! Neither is right. James got very angry about this and reminded us that everyone is to be treated the same. The fascination with the rich is just as bad as the disgust shown to the poor.

In our church today, poor people will not be asked to stand or to sit on the floor, but you might see:

- Someone who is without a home and doesn't smell very good being asked to sit in the back of the church.
- A rich person getting to spend more time with church leaders.
- A sermon saying that poor people are poor because they make bad choices and don't deserve help.

The truth is people are poor or rich for all sorts of reasons. But, if we are one body in Christ, we all belong to each other, and no one is better than anyone else. When you see someone who has a different amount of money than you, whether it is someone who has more or less, remember to treat them the same. No one is better than anyone else in Jesus.

LET'S TALK ABOUT IT

1 Have you ever worried about being left out because of something you have or don't have? How did that make you feel?

2 If a billionaire came to your house, how would they be treated? How about a person without a home? How can you make sure they would both be treated the same?

BE

BE FAITHFUL

For today, our fruit of the Spirit is faithfulness. Faithfulness is being loyal and true to your promises.

In the book of Acts, Luke wrote many things about churches, how they were started, and the early followers of Jesus. Paul and Timothy were two of those followers.

> Paul came to a city called Lystra and met a follower of Jesus whose name was Timothy. Timothy's mother was Jewish and his father was Greek.
>
> *—Acts 16:1 (paraphrase)*

Luke introduced us to Timothy by first talking about his background. Timothy's father was Greek, and at that time, Jewish people did not typically hang out with people who were not fully Jewish. But that didn't stop Paul from being friends with Timothy. In fact, Paul and Timothy soon began traveling together to other cities and telling all kinds of people about Jesus—Jewish people, Greek people, and people from other backgrounds as well (see Acts 16:4–6). When people saw Paul and Timothy walking, working, and worshiping God together as one, it helped them realize that God loves all kinds of people, and they should too. Paul and Timothy stayed friends and did many important things for Jesus. For as long as Paul lived, they remained faithful to one another. When we are faithful to our friends, we don't let them down. For instance, if people say mean things about them, we stand up for them and don't stop being their friend. This is called being loyal. Loyal is something Jesus wants us to be. In fact, one of the ways people know we are followers of Jesus is because we are loyal to Him. Jesus also wants us to be faithful and loyal to our friends, like Paul and Timothy were faithful to each other. It didn't matter to Paul that Timothy's mother was Jewish and his father was Greek. Paul wasn't looking only to be friends with people just like him, but also to be friends with people from different backgrounds, like Timothy. Since they both believed that Jesus was God, they had a special relationship. Later in life, Paul wrote letters to Timothy. Because they remained loyal to each other in good times and bad, we still remember Paul and Timothy today.

When we are faithful to our friends,
we don't let them down.

LET'S TALK ABOUT IT

1 Jesus expects us to have all kinds of friends and tell others about God's love even if they don't look like us or are from a different cultural background (see Matt. 28:19; Acts 1:8). Is there someone you know from a different background or culture that you would like to be friends with or tell about Jesus? Who is it? How might you become friends with them or tell them about Jesus?

2 Do you have a best or faithful friend? Who is it and why do you like being their friend?

INVITE OTHERS TO JOIN YOU

While Jesus was having dinner at his friend Matthew's house, many government officials that treated people unfairly, and other people that were not doing good things, came and ate with Jesus and his followers. In fact, Jesus invited them to do so! But when the religious leaders saw Jesus eating with those people, they were upset because they called those people "sinners" for not following God's rules the same way they did. The religious leader challenged Jesus' followers, "Why does your teacher eat with tax collectors and sinners?" One of the rules was that Jewish people should never be friends with sinners. But Jesus told the religious leaders that everyone needs to hear about God, to know that He loves them, and that no matter what bad things they have done in the past, God will forgive them so they can start over and live a better life in the future. This made the religious leaders mad. . . . but it's why so many people loved Jesus. He invited everyone to come and be with Him, no matter who they were or what they had done.

—*Matthew 9:10–12; Luke 15:1–7*
(paraphrase)

Is there anyone you know that someone has called a "bad person"? Has what others said about a person made you look at them suspiciously? How about a whole group of people? Have you ever been told that some groups of people are worse than others?

What Jesus showed the religious leaders is that everyone is loved by God—especially the people they excluded and called bad people. What's more, He wanted them to understand that none of us is really good. Jesus taught the religious leaders that they also needed God, even if they thought they didn't because they followed all of the rules.

Have you ever been told that some groups of people are worse than others?

Imagine if someone you know was having a birthday party, but they didn't invite you to come because someone said you are from a "bad" family. How would that make you feel? The truth is, none of us likes to be left out when others we know are eating, playing, or going somewhere fun together. It makes us feel like there's something wrong with us, like we're not good enough or as popular as everyone else that was invited to come. Even though it's not true that there's something wrong with us, still—not being included hurts our feelings.

When we are not included by others, we might begin thinking about or seeing ourselves in ways that are not true. This is very dangerous. The Bible tells us that God did not

make any mistakes when He created us. Each one of us is unique, which means we are special to God—not because we are like everyone else, but in fact, because we are not like anyone else. Yes, God wants you to try to be good, but no matter what, God loves you just the way you are!

LET'S TALK ABOUT IT

1 Were you ever not invited to attend a party, to do something, or to go somewhere, when other friends you know were asked to come? How did that make you feel? Later, how did you treat the person that did not invite you?

2 Now, think about a time when you were included and invited by someone else to do something, to attend a party, or to go somewhere. How did that make you feel? Later, how did you treat the person that invited you?

DO! Make a list of groups of people you've heard called "bad." Is this true about them? Now, write down ways God loves them.

KNOW

YOU HAVE AN ETERNAL DESIGN

When John was shown a vision of what it will be like in heaven, he saw all sorts of people worshiping God. It says there were people from every nation—men and women, Black and White, Latino and Asian. There was no one left out. They spoke different languages, but their song was the same!

Here is the new song they sang. "[Jesus] You are worthy to take the scroll and break open its seals. You are worthy because you were put to death. With your blood you bought people for God. They come from every tribe, people and nation, no matter what language they speak.

—Revelation 5:9

After this I looked, and there in front of me was a huge crowd of people. They stood in front of the throne and in front of the Lamb. There were so many that no one could count them. They came from every nation, tribe and people. That's true no matter what language they spoke. They were wearing white robes. In their hands they were holding palm branches.

—Revelation 7:9

Since the parts of your identity are
yours forever, take time to be
proud today of how God made you.

This beautiful vision shows us something important. Our ethnicities, our cultures, and the languages we speak are all part of our forever identities! That means these parts of us are not a mistake or unimportant. They are part of God's design.

Sometimes people will say we should try to be color blind. That when we focus on differences, we are just causing a fight. But that's not what we see in the Bible. If John had been color blind, he would not have pointed out the wonderful diversity in front of God's throne. If God had been color blind, He could have gotten rid of those differences. Instead, they are seen as beautiful. Since the parts of your identity are yours forever, take time to be proud today of how God made you. Look at the color of your skin and the texture of your hair, thanking God for them. Take time to be happy about the language you speak at home, even if it's not the language the other kids in your neighborhood speak. Be glad for the food you eat, even if it's not the same type of food served in your school cafeteria. God doesn't want us to forget our differences; God wants us to celebrate them and make sure everyone is treated equally despite them.

LET'S TALK ABOUT IT

1 The Bible says people from every tribe, tongue, and nation are represented around God's throne. In what ways would you describe your family's tribe, tongue, and nation?

2 Why are you glad your identity lasts forever? Knowing that, are there ways we should act differently now?

BE

BE JOYFUL

The last fruit of the Spirit we will talk about is joy. As we walk, work, and worship with all the different parts of the body, we all must give up some things for unity. When God asks us to sacrifice something, we want to be full of joy as we do it, not grumpy! Besides, it's not really a sacrifice, it's an exchange. When we give up anything for Jesus, we always get back more than we give!

If someone else thinks they have reasons to put confidence in the flesh, I have more: circumcised on the eighth day, of the people of Israel, of the tribe of Benjamin, a Hebrew of Hebrews; in regard to the law, a Pharisee; as for zeal, persecuting the church; as for righteousness based on the law, faultless. But whatever were gains to me I now consider loss for the sake of Christ. What is more, I consider everything a loss because of the surpassing worth of knowing Christ Jesus my Lord, for whose sake I have lost all things. I consider them garbage, that I may gain Christ.

—Philippians 3:4–8 (NIV)

The story of Paul in the Bible gives us a great example of this. Paul was a Jewish man. When the Church first began, Jewish folks sometimes thought of themselves as closer to God than others (but don't blame Jewish people for this—a couple hundred years later, Gentile people did the same thing!). The Jewish people were considered the leaders. This position of power led the Jewish people to look down on the Gentiles. Sometimes, they wouldn't even eat with them. Yet, Paul gave away this high position and instead served the Gentiles. He was even beaten and put in jail with them. What made the difference? Jesus.

High positions that we have because of things like our race or how much money we have become garbage when we know Jesus. Because he understood this, Paul had joy spending his life bringing Gentiles to Christ and living in unity within the Church.

LET'S TALK ABOUT IT

1 "None of you should look out just for your own good. Each of you should also look out for the good of others" (Phil. 2:4). What does this verse of Scripture mean to you? How can you live according to it?

2 What is one thing you might be able to joyfully give up to live in unity with others?

DO

EVERYONE MATTERS TO GOD . . . AND SHOULD MATTER TO YOU TOO!

For the past twenty readings, you have done the tough work of learning what the Bible teaches us on how to live together in unity. Now you're ready.

In video games, one of the best things is finding a cheat code. It makes everything so much easier. Well, now it's time to give you the super cheat code on how be one body (remember Jesus' prayer). Seriously. If you do this, it will take you from level one to level forty!

The parts that can be shown don't need special care. But God has put together all the parts of the body. And he has given more honor to the parts that didn't have any. In that way, the parts of the body will not take sides. All of them will take care of one another. If one part suffers, every part suffers with it. If one part is honored, every part shares in its joy.

—1 Corinthians 12:24–26

The New Testament book of 1 Corinthians is very helpful to us as we work for unity. Remember, Corinth was full of divisions between male and female, rich and poor, Jew and Gentile, followers of different leaders, and so many more. To that incredibly divided group, Paul wrote that they could have no division if they would give "more honor to the parts" that didn't have any.

So, how do you do that? A good example is the exodus of the Jewish people. In the exodus, thousands of enslaved people left Egypt to worship God. These people didn't leave in cars and trucks; they all had to walk, and some walked slower than others. Most groups of people would have let the slower people—perhaps children without families or disabled people—walk in the back. Back there, they might get attacked or left behind. This would separate the group. In Jewish tradition, however, God asked them to take anyone who might be at risk and put them in the middle. Another

name for people at risk is "marginalized," because they are literally on the margins or at the edges. When you put them in the middle, they are no longer marginalized, and the whole group sticks together. This may sound strange, but God asks that the best place in the group be given to the people who need it most. For most of this book, we've been talking about treating people equally. That is important. But the cheat code is treating people equitably—which simply means everyone has what they need to succeed. Take a look at the pictures above. Treating people equally is giving everyone a box, which is good. Treating people equitably means everyone gets the number of boxes they need to reach the apples, which is even better!

LET'S TALK ABOUT IT

1 In the Bible, there were three groups described as marginalized or at risk: the fatherless, the widow, and the immigrant. Why do you think these groups needed special care?

2 Where you live, who are those groups that are lacking honor or marginalized? Research this with your grown-up. Then discuss what you might do to make sure they have the honor they deserve, in church, or outside of church? What might you have to give up?

DO! Congratulations on finishing this book. We hope you have learned a lot about including others the way Jesus did! With your grown-up, write down one thing that you've learned and one thing that you want to do differently. Check back in a month to see if you've done what you said.

GLOSSARY

Kids and grown-ups, you can use this section to look up terms that you may not understand.

character—A patterns of thoughts, feelings, and actions.

church (small "c")—A local community of Christians who meet together regularly to pray, worship, and help each other.

Church (big "C")—People all over the world who are Christians.

Christian—Someone who has made God the boss of their life by believing that Jesus is the Son of God and following Him in what they do and say.

culture—The way a group of people does things, like their language, food, religion, or music.

ethnicity—Belonging to a group that shares the same ancestors (like great-great-great-grandparents) and has the same culture.

Jews—A group of people descended from a man named Israel (formerly called Jacob). They were picked by God to show the world who God is by living in a special way.

Gentile—Anyone who is not Jewish.

gentle—Having a kind and quiet nature. Not harsh.

Messiah—The leader God promised the Jewish people would save them. Jesus is the Messiah!

neutral—Not taking sides. Staying in the middle.

patient—Being willing to wait and not hurry.

peace—Having nothing broken and nothing missing in ourselves or our relationships.

poor—Not having everything that you need. Also called "destitute."

race—A group people are assigned to based on the color of their skin, their hair, and other parts of the way they look. These group labels are sometimes used to treat some people differently than others.

righteousness—Trying to make things right with God and with other people.

saints—Another word for a group of Christians.

unity—A feeling of togetherness; joining together to do something, sort of like a sports team that works together to win a game.

ABOUT
THE AUTHORS

A thought-leading writer and recognized champion of the Multiethnic Church Movement, Dr. Mark DeYmaz planted Mosaic Church (Little Rock, Arkansas) in 2001 where he remains the directional leader. In 2004, he cofounded the Mosaix Global Network and continues to serve as its CEO and president. Mark is the author of eight books including, *Building a Healthy Multi-ethnic Church and Disruption: Repurposing the Church to Redeem the Community*.

Dr. Oneya Fennell Okuwobi is teaching pastor at 21st Century Church, a church plant in Cincinnati, Ohio. She is also an assistant professor of sociology at the University of Cincinnati. Oneya's research examines how multiethnic churches and organizations can improve racial equity. She is married to Oladele and mom to Cadence, whose valuable feedback shaped this work.

Mark DeYmaz and
Oneya Fennell Okuwobi have also
written a book for grownups.

MULTIETHNIC CONVERSATIONS

AN EIGHT-WEEK JOURNEY TOWARD
UNITY IN YOUR CHURCH

MARK DeYMAZ and ONEYA FENNELL OKUWOBI

Multiethnic Conversations is a proven catalyst to help transform the minds, attitudes, and actions of people in your local church and lead them to enthusiastically embrace one another in the midst of cultural change. Structured around eight weeks of daily readings and thought-provoking questions, this attractive and accessible workbook is a Christ-centered, biblically accurate guide that facilitates authentic personal exploration and small group discussion of race, class, and culture. As the centerpiece tool of the Mosaix Global Network, this book brings diverse people together beyond the distinctions of this world that so often and otherwise divide. It all begins with conversation.

Published by Wesleyan Publishing House